MW01278352

The Day America Cried

Written by Dr. Teri J. Schwartz

Illustrated by Elena Dazé

Enduring Freedom Press
New York

Book Design, Cover Design & Image Research By:
Matthew L. Schwartz

Enduring Freedom Press
139-12 Coolidge Avenue
Briarwood, NY 11435
United States of America
http://www.efp.nypublish.com
efp@nypublish.com

Enduring Freedom Press, New York
© 2002 by Dr. Teri J. Schwartz
All rights reserved
Printed in the United States of America

1 3 5 7 9
 2 4 6 8 0

ISBN 0-9723945-0-8

Dedication

This book is dedicated to my children, Rachel, Michael and Daniel, and to children all over the world who, in uncertain times, have the courage to live, learn and continue to grow.

Acknowledgements

I am very grateful to my friend and colleague, Dr. Betsy Landau for her never-ending support, encouragement, technical assistance and orchestration in getting this book illustrated and published. I would like to thank Howard Landis, Oxford Lithograph, for printing this edition. A special thanks, wrapped in love, to my husband, Ray, for his ongoing belief in me.

Thanks to the writers of the Declaration of Independence and The Constitution as well as Abraham Lincoln for his Gettysburg Address portions of which appear in this book.

Dear Reader:

This is a story about the day America cried. Some of you may remember that day. Some of you were too little to have known about that day. Others of you were not yet born. It is a very sad story. If you can read this book all by yourself, you might want to have a grown-up read along with you so you can ask questions and talk about what happened.

Dr. Teri J. Schwartz

It was a beautiful warm morning. The sky was bright blue. Not a cloud was to be found. Children all over the United States of America were waking up and getting ready for school. It seemed like a typical sunny, September morning. Moms and dads were waking up their children. Some children were getting up by themselves. Breakfast was eaten. Backpacks were filled with notebooks and freshly sharpened pencils. Parents and children were heading out to start their day.

It was about a quarter to nine.
School-aged children had arrived at school
and begun their lessons. Some grown-ups
were at work. Many moms and dads,
brothers and sisters, aunts and uncles,
grandmas and grandpas, and friends were
on their way to work.

People who walked on the streets in
Manhattan looked up and saw an airplane.
It was a large jet plane. It was flying way
too low. Something was quite wrong.
Planes are not supposed to fly that low near
tall buildings. All of a sudden the jet
crashed into a very, very tall building. It
was one of the two buildings called the
World Trade Center.

The beautiful blue sky became black from the thick smoke. Children from nearby schools could see the fire and smoke. As people looked up at the very injured building, they wondered how this could have happened. Was it a terrible accident? Why else would an airplane have hit a building 107 floors tall? What had happened to the pilot? Was he sick? There is no way anyone would not see a building that tall. Was there something wrong with the plane?

Loud sirens were heard. Firefighters, police officers and paramedics rushed to the injured building. They ran up the stairs helping those who were hurt. They were telling people the safest and fastest way to get out of the building. Some people walked down as many as 90 flights of stairs to get out of the building. That's a lot of stairs.

Out on the streets near the building, people were running to find safe places away from the fire. Suddenly another big jet plane appeared in the sky. It flew around the injured building. It seemed to take aim. Then it crashed into the building next to it, the second building of the World Trade Center. There was more fire and smoke. The sky became so dark. It was hard for the people on the street to see where they were going. And it was hard to breathe.

Now we knew for sure. This was not a terrible accident. The two big planes were purposely crashed into these two buildings, the ones known as the twin towers of the World Trade Center. And America cried.

Who would fly planes into our beautiful buildings? Why would someone do such a bad thing? Who was being so mean to us?

People who were on the streets of Manhattan saw what happened and were very scared. Those who were walking down the stairs of the injured buildings were also scared. Many saw the burning twin towers on the television. They were also scared. And we were scared because we did not know whether more planes would be crashing into our tall buildings.

As rescue workers continued working to help the people out of the injured twin towers; as children in Washington, D. C. worked on math problems and reading, a plane circled overhead and crashed into the Pentagon. The Pentagon is a building that is not tall. It is very wide and has five sides. The Pentagon has offices for the military people who help the President of the United States make important decisions about what is best for America.

The sirens could now be heard all over Washington, D. C. and in New York City. America is very, very big. You could not hear the sirens all over America. Many children and grown-ups did not yet know about these plane crashes. They were at school or work. People in Washington, D. C. and in New York City called friends and family all over America to tell them they were okay. Also, people began to call friends and family in New York City and in Washington, D. C. to see if they were okay. People everywhere began to turn on their TVs and radios. For many days, the only show on every TV station would be the news about the plane crashes. The headlines on TV read America under Attack.

And America cried.

The President of the United States of America, George W. Bush, went on television to tell the people of America that something terrible had happened. People had stolen our airplanes and crashed them into important buildings. He called these people "terrorists."

President Bush immediately took action so that no more planes could be stolen and crashed into buildings. He told the airports to close down. He told the airplanes that were still flying to land immediately.

Before all the airplanes landed, one more jet plane fell from the sky in the state of Pennsylvania. This plane, too, had been stolen. The passengers on the plane had heard about the injured twin towers and the hurt Pentagon. They decided that they would not let their plane crash into another important building. They fought against the bad people who had stolen the airplane. They were very brave. They prevented another building from being hurt. However, in order to do that, they fought and caused the plane they were on to crash. Then the skies became silent on that beautiful September day. The sky was blue and clear. And America cried.

In New York City, Mayor Rudy Giuliani closed the bridges and tunnels. He wanted to make sure no one could hurt our bridges and tunnels. No cars could come into Manhattan. No cars could leave Manhattan. Subways stopped running. People could not travel around Manhattan by train. They could not travel in and out of Manhattan by train. No one could get into the subways and hurt them either. The telephones were not working very well. Some parents could not get through to their children's schools to comfort them. Other parents who worked near their children's schools came and took their children home to comfort them.

As the firefighters, police officers and paramedics helped people at the injured buildings; as news reporters talked to people near the twin towers; as Americans helped others in need, suddenly one of the twin towers collapsed. It was as if the building had too much weight at the top and could not hold itself up anymore. And America cried.

We all thought the firefighters would put out the fire. We all believed the injured building could be fixed. No one thought such a tall building would come falling down like a tower of blocks. Many sirens were heard. Many people rushed to the scene. Many people ran to places they hoped were safe.

Then, the other twin tower fell. All that was left of these two buildings were mounds of crumbled concrete and steel. As quickly as the towers fell, the firefighters placed an American flag at the top of the fallen towers. It was a message to the attackers. They might crush our towers, but America would not topple. Across America, throughout the day, many flags would be flown.

    Lots and lots of people worked in the
twin towers. It was the home of many
businesses. There was no warning that the
towers were about to fall down. Many
people who worked in those towers were
still inside. When the towers fell, many
people died. Some people lost moms or
dads, sisters and brothers, aunts and uncles
or grandparents. Many brave firefighters,
police officers and paramedics were still
trying to get people out of the buildings
when they fell. They had helped lots of
people get out of the twin towers before
they collapsed. But when the towers fell,
these brave firefighters, police officers and
paramedics died, too. It was so sad. And
America cried.

As the time passed on this Tuesday morning, the grown-ups who make the important decisions for our city, state and country were rushing around trying to make sure we were safe, that no other planes could crash into any building, anywhere in the United States of America. For days, the only planes that would fly over America would be jet fighter planes. They would be circling overhead to guard us. They would be there to protect us. Along the coastline, special ships would be watching over our shores making sure no ships could get close to America and hurt us.

In the face of these terrible events, Americans rushed to help each other. Some went down to ground zero, where the twin towers once stood. They served food. They brought clothing. The rescue workers were working around the clock. Some people just stood by and gave the rescue workers kind words and encouragement. Other people went to the hospitals and donated blood. People donated time, money and even places to sleep. Firefighters traveled from other states to help their [brother] New York City firefighters.

The people who lived near the twin towers would not be able to go back to their homes for a long time. It was too dangerous to return to their homes. Some of the buildings near the twin towers would collapse in the days to follow. Others were damaged and would be repaired once the fires from the fallen towers were put out. No one knew that day, September 11th, that it would be nearly 100 days before the fires would be put out for good.

Early on September 11th, people who worked in N. Y. C. had to find a way home. Some took ferries; some walked over bridges; others waited for the subways to run again. It was a long trip. Some grown-ups had to get their children from school before going home. As it became evening, neighbors called one another to see if everyone was safe. Most were. But thousands were not. Some friends and family members did not come home. Some were working at hospitals; some were working to put the fires out at ground zero and at the Pentagon. Sadly, some died when the plane hit the Pentagon; some died when the plane crashed in Pennsylvania; some died when the planes crashed into the twin towers.

    As the daylight disappeared across the horizon, people went to firehouses and lit candles. People went to ground zero and the Pentagon and lit candles, left flowers, wrote letters and put up photos of people lost on this terrible day. People would do this over and over in the months to come. Americans were creating memorials to remember those people whose lives were lost. People went to their churches, synagogues, mosques and temples to pray for America and to pray for those who died. And America cried.

Everyone began talking about healing. America had been hurt. We were sad. We were angry. We were scared. We needed to find ways to make us feel better. All over America, plans were being made for memorial and prayer services.

In New York City, a prayer service was going to take place in Yankee Stadium.

It was a beautiful, warm September morning and the world had changed for every American. President George W. Bush spoke to us on television. He said we would find out who did these terrible things and arrest them and punish them. The President was talking about those people who planned the plane crashes. Those who flew the planes died in the crashes. For many days, it was as if time stood still. Over and over the television would replay the crashes into the twin towers. Some people were glued to the TV for days. We were waiting to see what our President would do.

In the coming days, we bravely returned to our daily routines. Children went to school. Grown-ups went to work. We were afraid but we would not let those bad people break our spirit. More and more flags were flown. Flags were flown from cars. Posters with the American flag were placed in windows. People were wearing American flag pins, hats, shirts and scarves. Then came the hats and shirts with NYPD or FDNY. New Yorkers wanted their firefighters and police officers to know how much we appreciated them.

On that beautiful September 11th day, when the planes crashed, we did not have a clue as to why. We did not know who wanted to hurt us. We did not understand that some people do not like the friends we have. We did not know that some people were angry at us for keeping soldiers in their land after helping them when they were in trouble. It never occurred to us that people would not like us because of the freedoms we have.

Unless you are a Native American, an Indian or Eskimo, your family once lived somewhere else. If you or your parents were born in America, your grandparents or great-grandparents probably came from some other far away land. When your family came to America, they were hoping for a better life. The Pilgrims came because they could not freely practice their religion in England. Other people came because they thought America would provide them with the opportunity to make a better life for their families.

America takes pride in the freedoms we have. We can say what we want. We can even criticize the people who run America, like the President. We can dress the way we want. And we can choose to practice any religion in any way we choose. This is not so in many countries. People are not permitted to speak against their King or President. They must dress in a certain way and follow the rules for their religion that their ruler says is best.

There are many people in far away lands who are mad at Americans for the freedoms we have, the friends we keep and where our army bases have remained. Some of these people decided to teach us a lesson so they did mean things to us. They stole our jet planes and crashed them into our important buildings. We call these people "terrorists" because they try to scare us by suddenly attacking us without warning and attacking people who are not soldiers.

In the weeks to come, we would learn that the terrorists were fighting a Holy War for the sake of the Islamic religion. It was not an official war where one country declares war on another country. Not all Muslims believed what the terrorists were doing was right.

We were not used to attacks by terrorists. Many other countries, such as Israel and Ireland, are. President Bush would declare war on terrorism. He would ask other countries to help us to get rid of terrorism.

In the meantime, we became more careful and more alert. Life changed for all Americans. Our airports now had soldiers to protect us. Those flying would have to go through more security checks. Trucks had to be checked for bombs before going across bridges and tunnels. In New York City, there were many more police officers everywhere. And the F-16 jets were flying overhead.

It would be nearly four weeks before President Bush was ready to look for those people who planned the attack on America. He would send the Army, Navy, Air Force and Marines to a land very far away from America. This land is called Afghanistan. He and his advisors in the Pentagon believed that the people who planned these plane crashes lived in this land.

Americans were not mad at the people of Afghanistan. They wanted to capture the leaders who planned the attacks on our buildings and on us. They wanted to capture these terrorists so that they could have a trial and be punished. Our planes bombed the areas of Afghanistan where terrorists were thought to be. At the same time, other planes dropped food packages for the people of Afghanistan because they were hungry and in need of help.

We did not know on September 11th how long it would take to recover and heal. As the days and weeks passed, we resumed our usual activities. We were still scared or sad. Our life as an American had changed. But it was important to have Thanksgiving dinner. It is a symbol of the strength of the Pilgrims as they survived their first year in a new land, America. We would observe our holidays, be it Christmas, Chanukah, Kwanzaa or Ramadan.

We embraced a New Year, 2002.

But we would never forget. And we should never forget Tuesday, September 11, 2001. It is woven into the fabric we call American history. It is important to remember how brave we were, how we joined together in a time of need to help one another. It is important that we not forget the brave Americans who were not soldiers but died for their country.

A long time ago, a very famous President, Abraham Lincoln, spoke of soldiers who died in battle and asked Americans to remember them so that they "shall not have died in vain". And we have done this for our Americans who died on September 11th.

Dr. Teri J. Schwartz is a Clinical Psychologist who has been treating children, adults and families for over 20 years. She is also a child clinical supervisor at Steinway Child and Family Services in Howard Beach, New York. Her teaching and research activities at the undergraduate and graduate levels at Queens College and John Jay College of Criminal Justice of the City University of New York over the last seven years continues to be a source of enjoyment and enrichment. This is her first children's book although she has written professional articles.

Dr. Schwartz resides with her husband and three children in New York City.

For information about ordering additional copies of "The Day America Cried," or to find out more about the Enduring Freedom Press, please call us at our office: 718-263-8706 or visit our website at:

http://efp.nypublish.com